EMMANUEL JOSEPH

Diplomatic Warriors, The United States' Influence on Global Aid and Military Intervention

Copyright © 2025 by Emmanuel Joseph

All rights reserved. No part of this publication may be reproduced, stored or transmitted in any form or by any means, electronic, mechanical, photocopying, recording, scanning, or otherwise without written permission from the publisher. It is illegal to copy this book, post it to a website, or distribute it by any other means without permission.

First edition

This book was professionally typeset on Reedsy.
Find out more at reedsy.com

Contents

1 Chapter 1 — 1
2 Chapter 1: Introduction to Diplomatic Warriors — 3
3 Chapter 2: The Post-War Era and the Birth of Global Aid — 5
4 Chapter 3: The Cold War and Military Interventions — 7
5 Chapter 4: Humanitarian Interventions and Peacekeeping — 9
6 Chapter 5: The War on Terror and its Global Impact — 11
7 Chapter 6: The Role of Soft Power in Global Aid — 13
8 Chapter 7: The Pivot to Asia and its Implications — 15
9 Chapter 8: Human Rights and Democracy Promotion — 17
10 Chapter 9: The Middle East: Allies and Adversaries — 19
11 Chapter 10: Africa: Challenges and Opportunities — 21
12 Chapter 11: Latin America: Interventions and Partnerships — 23

1

Chapter 1

Introduction

The story of the United States on the global stage is one of unparalleled influence, marked by its unique approach to both aid and military intervention. This book delves into the intricacies of how the U.S., often seen as a beacon of democracy and freedom, has navigated the complex terrain of international relations. Through a historical and analytical lens, we will explore the motivations, strategies, and consequences of America's actions in various parts of the world. Our journey will reveal the delicate balance between the pursuit of national interests and the moral imperatives that have shaped U.S. foreign policy over the years.

From the aftermath of World War II to the present day, the United States has played a pivotal role in shaping the global order. The establishment of international institutions, such as the United Nations and NATO, underscored America's commitment to collective security and economic stability. However, this influence has not been without controversy. The U.S.'s involvement in conflicts, from the Vietnam War to the War on Terror, has sparked debates about the ethical implications and long-term effects of its military interventions. By examining these key events, we aim to provide a nuanced understanding of the complexities involved in U.S. foreign policy decisions.

Global aid has been another cornerstone of U.S. influence, reflecting its dual role as a benefactor and a strategic actor. Programs like the Marshall Plan and the President's Emergency Plan for AIDS Relief (PEPFAR) have showcased America's ability to mobilize resources for humanitarian causes. Yet, these initiatives are often intertwined with geopolitical objectives, revealing the intricate dance between altruism and strategic interests. This book will shed light on the impact of U.S. aid on recipient countries, exploring both the successes and the unintended consequences of these efforts.

Central to our exploration is the concept of soft power, a term coined by political scientist Joseph Nye. Soft power encompasses the ability of the United States to attract and persuade other nations through cultural diplomacy, economic assistance, and the promotion of democratic values. Through case studies and historical examples, we will examine how soft power has been wielded to complement traditional military and diplomatic strategies. The interplay between soft power and hard power will offer insights into the multifaceted nature of U.S. influence.

As we navigate through the chapters of this book, our goal is to provide a comprehensive and balanced perspective on the United States' role as a global power. By analyzing the past and present, we hope to contribute to a more informed discussion about the future of U.S. foreign policy. Ultimately, this book seeks to illuminate the path of the diplomatic warriors who have shaped and continue to shape the United States' influence on global aid and military intervention.

2

Chapter 1: Introduction to Diplomatic Warriors

From the signing of the Treaty of Paris in 1783 to the recent challenges in the Middle East, the United States has continually evolved into a pivotal player on the global stage. This chapter sets the scene by exploring the foundational principles that have guided U.S. diplomacy and military intervention over the centuries. Through a historical lens, we'll trace the roots of the United States' foreign policy and its inherent philosophy of promoting democracy, ensuring stability, and protecting its national interests abroad. Our journey begins with the key moments that have shaped U.S. strategy, from the Monroe Doctrine to the Roosevelt Corollary.

A deep dive into the ideological underpinnings reveals how the concepts of Manifest Destiny and American exceptionalism have influenced the nation's approach to international relations. This chapter examines the balance between isolationism and interventionism, illustrating the internal and external pressures that have swayed American policy decisions. By understanding these foundational elements, readers will gain insight into the intricate web of motivations that drive the U.S. to act on the global stage.

Furthermore, we will explore the role of key figures in the formulation of U.S. foreign policy. From early statesmen like Thomas Jefferson and John Quincy Adams to contemporary leaders such as Madeleine Albright and

Condoleezza Rice, the chapter highlights their contributions and the lasting impact of their policies. Their decisions, often controversial and far-reaching, provide a rich tapestry of lessons on leadership and international diplomacy.

The chapter concludes with a reflection on the dual nature of U.S. influence—both as a beacon of hope and a source of contention. By acknowledging the complexities and contradictions in America's global role, we set the stage for a deeper exploration of the subsequent chapters. The journey of understanding the United States' influence on global aid and military intervention begins here, with a nuanced perspective on its diplomatic warriors.

3

Chapter 2: The Post-War Era and the Birth of Global Aid

The aftermath of World War II marked a significant turning point in global politics and international relations. In this chapter, we delve into the establishment of major international organizations, such as the United Nations and the Bretton Woods institutions, which were instrumental in shaping the post-war order. The United States emerged as a superpower, driven by a vision of global cooperation and economic recovery. The Marshall Plan, a cornerstone of this vision, exemplified the U.S.'s commitment to rebuilding war-torn Europe and preventing the spread of communism.

The chapter explores the strategic objectives behind the U.S.'s global aid initiatives, highlighting the interplay between humanitarian efforts and geopolitical considerations. The Marshall Plan, for instance, was not merely an act of benevolence but a calculated move to create a stable and prosperous Europe that could resist Soviet influence. By examining the successes and limitations of these early aid programs, we gain a better understanding of the complexities involved in international assistance.

We also take a closer look at the role of American non-governmental organizations (NGOs) and private foundations in global aid efforts. Institutions like the Ford Foundation and the Rockefeller Foundation played a crucial role in promoting education, health, and agricultural development in developing countries. Their contributions, often in partnership with governmental initiatives, helped lay the groundwork for modern international aid frameworks.

The chapter concludes by addressing the criticism and controversies that have accompanied U.S. global aid efforts. While the intention behind these programs was often noble, the implementation faced numerous challenges, including accusations of paternalism and neocolonialism. By acknowledging these critiques, we pave the way for a more balanced and informed discussion in the subsequent chapters.

4

Chapter 3: The Cold War and Military Interventions

The Cold War era was characterized by intense rivalry between the United States and the Soviet Union, leading to numerous military interventions across the globe. In this chapter, we explore the ideological battle that defined this period and the ways in which the U.S. sought to contain the spread of communism. The doctrine of containment, as articulated by George F. Kennan, became the cornerstone of U.S. foreign policy, guiding its actions in regions as diverse as Latin America, Southeast Asia, and the Middle East.

The chapter provides a detailed analysis of key military interventions, such as the Korean War, the Vietnam War, and the Bay of Pigs invasion. Each case study highlights the strategic objectives, the challenges faced, and the outcomes of these interventions. By examining the decision-making processes and the role of key political and military leaders, we gain a deeper understanding of the complexities and consequences of U.S. actions during the Cold War.

In addition to direct military interventions, the chapter also delves into covert operations and proxy wars. The CIA's involvement in regime change efforts in countries like Iran and Guatemala underscores the clandestine nature of the U.S.'s struggle against communist influence. These covert actions, often shrouded in secrecy, had far-reaching implications for the countries involved and for U.S. foreign policy as a whole.

The chapter concludes by reflecting on the human cost of these military interventions. The loss of lives, the displacement of populations, and the long-term socio-economic impacts serve as a sobering reminder of the price of ideological conflict. By acknowledging these consequences, we set the stage for a more critical examination of the U.S.'s role in global military interventions in the following chapters.

5

Chapter 4: Humanitarian Interventions and Peacekeeping

While the Cold War era was dominated by military interventions driven by ideological considerations, the post-Cold War period saw a shift towards humanitarian interventions and peacekeeping efforts. In this chapter, we explore the changing nature of U.S. involvement in global conflicts and crises. The concept of the "Responsibility to Protect" (R2P) emerged as a guiding principle, emphasizing the moral obligation to intervene in situations where human rights were at risk.

The chapter examines key humanitarian interventions, such as the U.S.-led intervention in Somalia, the NATO intervention in Kosovo, and the multinational efforts in Bosnia and Herzegovina. Each case study highlights the challenges and complexities involved in balancing the need for immediate humanitarian assistance with the long-term goal of sustainable peace and stability. The role of international organizations, such as the United Nations and NATO, in facilitating these interventions is also explored.

We also delve into the debates surrounding the legitimacy and effectiveness of humanitarian interventions. While some argue that such interventions are necessary to prevent atrocities and protect vulnerable populations, others contend that they can lead to unintended consequences and undermine national sovereignty. By examining these debates, we gain a more nuanced understanding of the ethical and practical considerations involved in humanitarian interventions.

The chapter concludes by reflecting on the lessons learned from past humanitarian interventions. The successes and failures of these efforts provide valuable insights into the complexities of global peacekeeping and the challenges of building a more just and peaceful world. These lessons will inform our discussion of contemporary U.S. military and aid strategies in the subsequent chapters.

6

Chapter 5: The War on Terror and its Global Impact

The events of September 11, 2001, marked a watershed moment in U.S. foreign policy, leading to the launch of the War on Terror. In this chapter, we explore the origins, objectives, and implications of this global campaign against terrorism. The U.S. response to the 9/11 attacks, including the invasion of Afghanistan and the subsequent intervention in Iraq, reshaped the geopolitical landscape and had far-reaching consequences for international relations.

The chapter provides an in-depth analysis of the key military and diplomatic strategies employed in the War on Terror. From the use of drone strikes and targeted killings to the establishment of detention facilities like Guantanamo Bay, we examine the methods used to combat terrorist networks and the ethical dilemmas they present. The role of intelligence agencies, such as the CIA and the NSA, in gathering and analyzing information is also discussed.

We also explore the impact of the War on Terror on global aid and development efforts. The U.S. focus on counterterrorism has led to a reallocation of resources towards security and military initiatives, often at the expense of humanitarian and development programs. This shift has had significant implications for countries receiving U.S. aid, as well as for the broader international aid community.

The chapter concludes by reflecting on the long-term consequences of the War on Terror. The rise of new terrorist organizations, the destabilization of regions like the Middle East and North Africa, and the erosion of civil liberties in the name of security are some of the enduring legacies of this global campaign. By acknowledging these consequences, we set the stage for a more critical examination of the U.S.'s role in global aid and military intervention in the following chapters.

7

Chapter 6: The Role of Soft Power in Global Aid

The concept of soft power, coined by Joseph Nye, has become an integral part of U.S. foreign policy, especially in the realm of global aid. In this chapter, we explore how the United States uses cultural diplomacy, economic assistance, and educational exchange programs to influence other nations and promote its values. By leveraging soft power, the U.S. aims to build alliances, foster goodwill, and create an environment conducive to its strategic interests.

We examine key initiatives, such as the Fulbright Program, the Peace Corps, and USAID's development projects, to understand how these efforts contribute to the U.S.'s global influence. These programs not only provide tangible benefits to recipient countries but also serve as a means of projecting American ideals and strengthening bilateral relationships. The chapter also highlights the role of American popular culture, including Hollywood, music, and sports, in shaping global perceptions of the United States.

The chapter delves into the challenges and limitations of soft power. While cultural diplomacy and economic assistance can build positive relationships, they can also be met with skepticism and resistance. The effectiveness of soft power often depends on the credibility and consistency of the U.S.'s actions, as well as the ability to address the needs and aspirations of the target audience.

By analyzing these factors, we gain a more comprehensive understanding of the complexities of soft power in global aid.

The chapter concludes by reflecting on the evolving nature of soft power in the digital age. With the rise of social media and the internet, the U.S. has new tools at its disposal to engage with global audiences. However, these technological advancements also pose new challenges, such as the spread of misinformation and the competition for attention in an increasingly crowded information landscape. By exploring these dynamics, we set the stage for a deeper discussion of contemporary U.S. foreign policy in the following chapters.

8

Chapter 7: The Pivot to Asia and its Implications

In recent years, the U.S. has shifted its strategic focus towards the Asia-Pacific region, recognizing its growing economic and geopolitical significance. This chapter explores the "Pivot to Asia" policy, initiated during the Obama administration, and its implications for global aid and military intervention. The policy aims to strengthen U.S. alliances, enhance regional security, and promote economic integration in the Asia-Pacific.

We examine key components of the Pivot to Asia, including the Trans-Pacific Partnership (TPP), the enhancement of military presence in the region, and increased diplomatic engagement with Asian countries. The chapter highlights the strategic importance of allies such as Japan, South Korea, and Australia, as well as the challenges posed by emerging powers like China and India. By analyzing these dynamics, we gain a deeper understanding of the U.S.'s efforts to maintain its influence in a rapidly changing region.

The chapter also delves into the impact of the Pivot to Asia on global aid efforts. The U.S. has increased its development assistance to countries in the Asia-Pacific, focusing on areas such as infrastructure, health, and education. These initiatives aim to promote stability and economic growth, while also countering China's growing influence through its Belt and Road Initiative. By examining these aid programs, we gain insights into the strategic objectives and outcomes of the U.S.'s engagement in the region.

The chapter concludes by reflecting on the challenges and opportunities of the Pivot to Asia. The U.S.'s ability to navigate complex regional dynamics, build enduring partnerships, and address the concerns of its allies will be crucial to the success of this policy. By acknowledging these factors, we set the stage for a more nuanced discussion of U.S. foreign policy in the Asia-Pacific in the subsequent chapters.

9

Chapter 8: Human Rights and Democracy Promotion

Promoting human rights and democracy has long been a cornerstone of U.S. foreign policy. In this chapter, we explore the ways in which the U.S. seeks to advance these values through global aid and military intervention. From supporting democratic movements to condemning authoritarian regimes, the U.S. has employed a range of strategies to promote human rights and democratic governance around the world.

We examine key initiatives, such as the National Endowment for Democracy (NED) and the State Department's Bureau of Democracy, Human Rights, and Labor (DRL), to understand how the U.S. supports civil society organizations, political parties, and independent media in various countries. These efforts aim to strengthen democratic institutions, promote political participation, and protect fundamental freedoms. The chapter also highlights the role of American diplomacy in advocating for human rights at international forums, such as the United Nations Human Rights Council.

The chapter delves into the challenges and controversies surrounding U.S. democracy promotion efforts. While these initiatives often have noble intentions, they can also be perceived as interference in the internal affairs of other countries. The effectiveness of democracy promotion depends on the ability to tailor strategies to local contexts and build genuine partnerships with local actors. By examining these factors, we gain a more nuanced understanding of the complexities of promoting human rights and democracy.

The chapter concludes by reflecting on the evolving landscape of human rights and democracy promotion in the 21st century. The rise of authoritarianism, the impact of digital technology, and the changing nature of global power dynamics pose new challenges and opportunities for the U.S. By exploring these trends, we set the stage for a deeper discussion of contemporary U.S. foreign policy in the following chapters.

10

Chapter 9: The Middle East: Allies and Adversaries

The Middle East has long been a focal point of U.S. foreign policy, characterized by a complex web of alliances and adversarial relationships. In this chapter, we explore the strategic importance of the region and the ways in which the U.S. has sought to influence its political and security dynamics. From securing energy resources to countering extremist groups, the U.S. has a range of interests that drive its engagement in the Middle East.

We examine key military interventions, such as the Gulf War, the Iraq War, and the ongoing conflict in Syria, to understand the objectives, challenges, and outcomes of U.S. actions in the region. The chapter also highlights the role of diplomacy in managing relationships with key allies, such as Israel, Saudi Arabia, and Egypt, as well as navigating the complexities of adversarial relationships with countries like Iran.

The chapter delves into the impact of U.S. aid programs in the Middle East. From economic assistance to security cooperation, the U.S. has invested significant resources in promoting stability and development in the region. However, these efforts often face challenges, including political instability, corruption, and anti-American sentiment. By examining these factors, we gain a deeper understanding of the complexities of U.S. engagement in the

Middle East.

The chapter concludes by reflecting on the future of U.S. policy in the region. The shifting geopolitical landscape, the rise of new regional powers, and the evolving nature of global threats pose new challenges and opportunities for the U.S. By acknowledging these dynamics, we set the stage for a more nuanced discussion of contemporary U.S. foreign policy in the Middle East in the following chapters.

11

Chapter 10: Africa: Challenges and Opportunities

A frica presents a unique set of challenges and opportunities for U.S. foreign policy, characterized by a diverse array of political, economic, and security dynamics. In this chapter, we explore the ways in which the U.S. has sought to engage with the continent, from promoting economic development to addressing security threats. The chapter highlights the strategic importance of Africa in the context of global aid and military intervention.

We examine key initiatives, such as the President's Emergency Plan for AIDS Relief (PEPFAR), the Millennium Challenge Corporation (MCC), and the African Growth and Opportunity Act (AGOA), to understand how the U.S. supports economic growth, health, and governance in African countries. These programs aim to address the root causes of poverty and instability, while also promoting trade and investment opportunities for American businesses.

The chapter also delves into the challenges of U.S. engagement in Africa. Issues such as corruption, political instability, and weak institutions pose significant obstacles to the success of aid programs. Additionally, the growing influence of other global powers, such as China and Russia, presents new challenges for U.S. policy in the region. By examining these factors, we gain a more comprehensive understanding of the complexities of U.S. engagement in Africa.

The chapter concludes by reflecting on the future of U.S.-Africa relations. The continent's dynamic demographic and economic trends present both opportunities and challenges for the U.S. By acknowledging these dynamics, we set the stage for a deeper discussion of contemporary U.S. foreign policy in Africa in the following chapters.

12

Chapter 11: Latin America: Interventions and Partnerships

Latin America has historically been a region of significant interest for U.S. foreign policy, characterized by a complex mix of interventions and partnerships. In this chapter, we explore the strategic importance of Latin America and the ways in which the U.S. has sought to influence its political and economic landscape. From the Monroe Doctrine to the War on Drugs, U.S. engagement in Latin America has evolved over time, reflecting changing priorities and challenges.

We examine key military and covert interventions, such as the interventions in Cuba, Chile, and Nicaragua, to understand the objectives, challenges, and outcomes of U.S. actions in the region. The chapter also highlights the role of diplomacy and economic assistance in fostering partnerships with key allies, such as Mexico, Colombia, and Brazil. By analyzing these dynamics, we gain a deeper understanding of the U.S.'s efforts to promote stability and economic development in Latin America.

The chapter delves into the impact of U.S. aid programs in Latin America. From development assistance to security cooperation, the U.S. has invested significant resources in addressing issues such as poverty, drug trafficking, and governance. However, these efforts often face challenges, including corruption, political instability, and anti-American sentiment. By examining these factors, we gain a more comprehensive understanding of the complexities of U.S. engagement in Latin America.

The chapter concludes by reflecting on the future of U.S.-Latin America relations. The region's dynamic political and economic trends present both opportunities and challenges for the U.S. By acknowledging these dynamics, we set the stage for a more nuanced discussion of contemporary U.S. foreign policy in Latin America in the final chapter.

Chapter 12: The Future of U.S. Influence on Global Aid and Military Intervention

As we look to the future, the role of the United States in global aid and military intervention continues to evolve in response to new challenges and opportunities. In this concluding chapter, we reflect on the key themes and lessons from the previous chapters, and explore the future trajectory of U.S. foreign policy. The chapter addresses the changing geopolitical landscape, the rise of new global powers, and the impact of technological advancements on international relations.

We examine the potential for new forms of international cooperation and multilateralism, as well as the challenges posed by emerging threats such as climate change, cyber warfare, and global pandemics. The chapter highlights the importance of adapting U.S. foreign policy to address these complex and interconnected issues, while also promoting stability, democracy, and human rights.

The chapter also delves into the role of domestic politics in shaping U.S. foreign policy. The influence of public opinion, interest groups, and political leadership on foreign policy decisions is explored, highlighting the dynamic interplay between domestic and international factors. By understanding these dynamics, we gain insights into the potential direction of U.S. foreign policy in the coming years.

The chapter concludes by reflecting on the enduring principles that have guided U.S. engagement on the global stage. The commitment to promoting democracy, ensuring stability, and protecting national interests remains central to U.S. foreign policy, even as the methods and strategies evolve. By acknowledging the complexities and contradictions in America's global

CHAPTER 11: LATIN AMERICA: INTERVENTIONS AND PARTNERSHIPS

role, we set the stage for a more informed and balanced discussion of its future influence on global aid and military intervention.

In the end, the United States' role as a diplomatic warrior on the global stage is shaped by a combination of historical legacies, strategic objectives, and ethical considerations. As the world continues to change, the U.S. will need to navigate these challenges with a renewed commitment to its core values and a willingness to adapt to new realities. By understanding the past and present of U.S. influence on global aid and military intervention, we can better anticipate the future and contribute to a more just and peaceful world.

Diplomatic Warriors: The United States' Influence on Global Aid and Military Intervention is a comprehensive examination of America's role on the world stage, unraveling the intricate web of motivations, strategies, and consequences of its actions. This book delves into the dual aspects of U.S. influence: global aid and military intervention, providing a balanced and nuanced perspective on its foreign policy decisions.

Through twelve captivating chapters, readers will journey from the aftermath of World War II to the present day, exploring pivotal moments that have defined U.S. diplomacy. From the Marshall Plan to the War on Terror, each chapter offers an in-depth analysis of America's humanitarian efforts and military engagements, shedding light on both the successes and controversies that have accompanied these initiatives.

Central to the narrative is the concept of soft power, highlighting how the United States has used cultural diplomacy, economic assistance, and the promotion of democratic values to shape global perceptions. The book examines the interplay between soft power and hard power, providing insights into the multifaceted nature of U.S. influence.

By exploring key case studies and historical examples, **Diplomatic Warriors** offers readers a comprehensive understanding of the complexities involved in U.S. foreign policy. The book aims to contribute to a more informed discussion about the future of America's role in global aid and military intervention, ultimately illuminating the path of the diplomatic warriors who have shaped and continue to shape the United States' influence around the world.

www.ingramcontent.com/pod-product-compliance
Lightning Source LLC
LaVergne TN
LVHW010445070526
838199LV00066B/6202